BOATMAN
Ashe Vernon

Copyright © 2016 Ashe Vernon

All rights reserved. No part of this book may be reproduced or performed without the author's written consent, except for quotations in articles and reviews.

Cover art by the late Mark Vernon, photographed and edited by Christopher Diaz.

Internal illustrations by Kelsey Schreck.

FIRST EDITION

ISBN: 1534637230
ISBN-13: 978-1534637238

To Dad.
I know you'd have done things differently
if you could.

CONTENTS

Enter George	1
The Boatman of the River Styx	2
Word of Mouth #1	3
A Beginning Shaped Like an Ending	4
Introduction	5
The Boat That Is Too Big or Too Wide	6
A Conversation	7
The River	8
Word of Mouth #2	9
Jars of Fireflies	10
Being Alive	12
The Suicide Note George Didn't Write	14
Runs In the Family	15
He Is a Half-Step Out of Time	16
Oh, He Hates Her	18
Splinter	20
Word of Mouth #3	21
Olive Branch	22
Q&A	23
The Voicemail	24
The Suicide Note That Doesn't Look Like One	25
Into the Blue	26
The Boatman's Monologue	28
How to Comfort a Man Who Has Never Been Human	30
Word of Mouth #4	32
Finished	34
Kharon, of the River	35
Past, Present, Future	36
Into the Blue pt 2	38
Word of Mouth #5	40
Postscript	42
	43

"A small mercy from the universe: the comfort of knowing loneliness is still a shared condition."

Natalie Wee

ENTER GEORGE

If the story even has a beginning, then it has to be George.
And if George has a beginning, it isn't in a hospital
or an elementary school. It isn't in her mother's arms or
her first apartment or tucked away inside the walls
of a confessional.
It's on the docks, near her parents' home:
where her grandmother said never to play,
where the fog hasn't lifted for three generations,
where she shed what was left of her childhood
and never even heard it hit the ground.

Plenty of children grow up too quickly.

Imagine George: beautiful and baby faced,
dropping beads of childhood like a broken strand of pearls.
Imagine that they gleam clear and bright on the water,
bobbing in the surf. Long gone before she ever
thought to look for them.

And after twenty more years in the shadow of an ache
she doesn't know the name of, she finds herself back
at the mouth of that same shoreline
wanting nothing more than to be
swallowed by it.

THE BOATMAN OF THE RIVER STYX

The boatman is a carpenter.

He's been in this business for longer
than anyone can remember. He has met
everyone who has ever mattered and everyone
who will ever matter and
everyone who won't.

He built their boats for them.

But the dead
never have anything
interesting to say.

WORD OF MOUTH #1

George's grandmother said,
There's something old in that water.

The old fisherman at the end of the docks said,
*There's never nobody there, but some days
you can feel eyes followin' you.*

Big Jimmy said,
*These boats come and go and they ain't got
no names on 'em. No passengers. They pull up
outta the water like they're being captained
by a ghost.*

Madi Mae said,
*When the mist gets thick, you can hear someone
building. Hammers and saws on wood. Coming from
nowhere. Coming from the water herself.*

In the town library, clippings from yellowed newspapers
make it seem like this has been going on
for a long, long time now.

A BEGINNING SHAPED LIKE AN ENDING

Twenty years changes a place, but not the docks.
They stand exactly as she remembers them: ghostly and
insubstantial compared to the wash of the sea.
All that horizon and the scuffle of the fishermen
in the early hours of the morning when the world
has no business being awake.

We've missed so much of George's story. See,
it didn't happen here, but it was heavy.
Too much to carry.
And the docks are the first breath of life
that George can remember, so she came back
for the sake of symmetry. She came here
to give all that aching
to the sea.

And then the boatman, perched on the same pier
that he has kept for generations: its rotted planks peeking out
from the mist like something unearthly.
He is mostly a man,
but not quite—
with his mouth that never moves,
with his too long legs, with his too big eyes,
with a body that seems all at once impossibly old
and entirely new: untouched by weather or time,
as though he'd spent eternity in a glass display case
at a museum.

She remembers him.

INTRODUCTION

When she sits down beside him and
kicks her feet in the water
he doesn't look at her.
People don't come here for him.

I'm George.

He is hammer and wood.
Today is for the boat that's shaped like
nobody. The boat that is too big or too wide
or else, off-balance.
He has never gotten this far into a boat
without knowing who it is who'd be dying.

Do you have a name?

A riddle: what good is a name
to a man who has no one to call him by it?
He is the boatman; he has been for centuries.
If he was ever anything more, he's forgotten.

Who are the boats for?

A spark of a memory: a little girl, with light
dripping off her like pearls into the water.
A mason jar of fireflies tucked where no one
will ever find it.
She can see the boats.

Funny, you didn't ask if I could see you.

But everyone can see him.
It's just that nobody ever wants to.

THE BOAT THAT IS TOO BIG OR TOO WIDE

The boatman has built a boat for every soul
who's ever crossed the Styx.
Maybe
he's building yours.
And anyway, he will.
He always does.

No boat is ever the same,
but this boat,
this boat is—

wrong.

It belongs to no one.
In three thousand years of building,
there has never been a boat like this.

A CONVERSATION

Boatman of what?

> **The River Styx.**

Wait, but does that mean that this—
this is the river?

> **No, this is the ocean.**

Hilarious.
You build your boats here,
but I don't see any rivers.

> **You're looking for rivers in the wrong places.**

I'm not looking for rivers.
But
if I were,
where would I start?

> **It's not so hard to see, at night.**
> **Not in a small town like this.**
> **the lights don't blot it out, here.**

The Milky Way? That's the river?

> **Is that what you call it?**

Well, I don't call it a river.

> **You would if you made your boats right.**

THE RIVER

The river was different, before—
back when Hades and his Underworld
were fact
instead of bedtime story.
Back when Zeus was still the kind of god
that people prayed to.

But the power moved.
The stories changed.
The prayers were offered up
to other gods in other places
and Olympus
and Hades
fell into decay.
But the river—

The river remained.

WORD OF MOUTH #2

George's grandmother said,
I saw him once. The man who builds the boats.
he was—wrong. All leg. All eyes. He was
shaped like a man,
but he wasn't one.

George's father said,
Stop telling stories. You're scaring her.

George's grandmother said,
She should be scared. She should stay away
from that man.

George, still eight years old and bright and glowing, said,
There are lots of men at the harbor, Grandma.

Not like this one, baby.
Not like this one.

JARS OF FIREFLIES

The next morning, the ocean is so still
it doesn't look like an ocean. And the boatman
isn't building, and so doesn't look
like the boatman. Instead,
he sits near the water and cradles
a swaddle of cloth to his chest.

They're yours.

Again, he speaks without speaking:
never opens his mouth. She supposes—
well, she should be frightened, shouldn't she?
Of the way his voice seems to come from the water?
Or the mist?
But sitting down beside him seems the most
natural thing in the world.
(Imagine, a woman like her
making friends with death.)

You left them on my harbor.

Beneath black velvet: mason jars
full of fireflies, except—
too bright. Too perfectly round.
Like a broken strand of pearls
turned alive, turned bioluminescent
and buzzing.

They remember you.

BEING ALIVE

The problem is, there's no putting childhood back
in a body that's outgrown it. There's no room.
George holds the jars in her hands, but they don't
feel like they belong to her. Not anymore.

The boatman stares with those big, bug eyes.
Otherworldly. Unblinking.
Waiting.
Waiting for what?

She sets them down. Says,
I must seem like an infant to you.

He snatches the jars back: holds them the way a mother
holds a frightened child, like he can't believe she'd
abandon them, like this is something so much bigger
than the firefly jars.
For the first time, when he speaks,
he moves his mouth.

His voice, like a rusty hinge sealed shut with disuse,
spills from him as nothing more than a whisper of seafoam:

You've barely been born.

I've wanted to die.

But you haven't even lived.

Neither have you.

I'm older than anything you have ever touched.

12

But what are you afraid of?

I'm not afraid of anything.

You aren't alive, then.

Why does being alive mean being afraid?

I don't know. It just does.

THE SUICIDE NOTE GEORGE DIDN'T WRITE BUT ALMOST DID
(or did write but shoved into the bottom of her sock drawer in case she ever needed it)

Dear Mom and Dad,

It's not like I'm the only kid who ever had to grow up too fast, you know? I don't want you to feel like you were bad parents. It's nobody's fault. Nobody made me like this. My brain's just fucked up.

I want you to know that I know you did your best. Sorry for all the jokes I made about dying that weren't really jokes but were still supposed to be funny. I know you weren't laughing.

The thing is, you can get everything you're supposed to want in life and still be unhappy. That probably makes me ungrateful. I don't mean to be. They say it's all chemical, right?

This isn't your fault, alright? It isn't. And I'm sorry that after all this time, I'm still making you clean up after me.

Forever,
your Georgie

RUNS IN THE FAMILY

George's mother hanged herself.

They say depression is hereditary.
They say women have always carried pain
that doesn't belong to them. They say
there are thousands of years of weight
to be shouldered and women's shoulders are just
so
soft.

George has always loved the ocean.
She keeps thinking that maybe,
if there isn't a body,
her father won't take it so hard.

HE IS A HALF-STEP OUT OF TIME

The boatman is a carpenter.

He has met
everyone who has ever mattered and everyone
who will ever matter and
everyone who won't.

(George's mother mattered. She cried when he
sent her out to the Styx, but he couldn't tell if it was
sorrow or relief that had her sobbing.)

The boat is still not done.
It is too big, or too wide,
or else, off balance.
Every time he starts to understand
the soul meant to inhabit it,
he drives in a new nail and the whole thing
st—
stutters.

He is terrified,
(if terror is even something he is capable of)
that this boat might
be George's.

OH, HE HATES HER

What did my mother say, when you met her?

George was three states away, when her mother died,
but she can still remember how her father collapsed
into rubble and silt on the telephone: how he spilled
and spilled and spilled until he was caught in every
crack in the floor. She remembers an unending plane ride
and showing up at the house she was raised in
only to sweep him out from under the table and
put him back together. Sort of.
He never truly recovered.

They say depression is hereditary, and
George was a grown woman before she truly
understood her mother: all her quiet
breaking and unbreaking, the tenderness
she balanced on like porcelain stilts.

Was she happy? Is it–better?

For the boatman, fear feels like this:
a clenched fist where his throat used to be.
His heart pushed from his mouth and
rolling toward the water. Hurricane force winds
running parallel to his spine.
He goes still as—
Well. Still as death
when she asks him that.

Do you know how many souls I see?
I don't remember your mother.

George, she doesn't stop pushing. She leans in,
and oh, she is warm in all the ways he
never will be and oh, he hates her for it. She says,
I don't believe you. I bet you remember all of them.

And he does. And three thousand years of memory
is a heavy weight to carry, yet he never felt tired
until he met her.

Come on, boatman! You know why I'm here.
Give me something to look forward to.

He thinks of the boat: too big, too wide.
He thinks how much George looks like her mother.
He stops thinking.
He earthquakes.
GET OUT.
LEAVE ME ALONE—
I JUST WANT TO BE LEFT ALONE.
DON'T COME BACK,
YOU STUPID LITTLE GIRL,
DON'T EVER COME BACK.

She stumbles.
She goes.

SPLINTER

Wooden boat meets two thousand years of suppressed heartache.
It screams when the boatman doesn't know how to:
buckles under the hammer.
Again and again and again and again.
There's something familiar to that kind of splinter.
Who belongs to a thing so broken?
No one. No one does and no one ever will and
he hates this boat, he hates it, he hates it, he hates it.
(Wrong, the boat is wrong.)
The boat is nothing, now: just a catastrophe of almost.
A skeleton left behind where an ending could have been.

WORD OF MOUTH #3

George's grandmother said,
*The fog over that harbor never lifts. Have you noticed? In town,
there's not a cloud in the sky, but the docks—
they're always murky.*

The old fisherman at the end of the docks said,
*Oh, I grew up on these waters, I'm not afraid of 'em.
Every old place has its ghost stories.
Still,
you wouldn't catch me here alone after moonrise.*

Big Jimmy said,
*You just don't go playin' with things you don't understand,
you just don't do it. There're things we're supposed to know,
in this world, and there's things we just ain't.
Whatever's out on that water?
We're not s'posed to know about that one.*

Madi Mae said,
*My daddy died in that harbor. Drowned,
not fifteen feet from land. Now, I'm not sayin'
it was because of that thing what lives there, but—
well it didn't save him either, now did it?*

OLIVE BRANCH

You know, you're not exactly easy to be friends with.

A half-step out of time, it's impossible for the boatman to say
just how many days he's been without her. Or weeks.
They stand, the wreckage of a would-be boat between them
and the boatman knows he's supposed to speak, but he,
like the dead, has nothing to say.

This mess isn't the boat, is it?

He'd expected he wouldn't see her again until
he shook hands with her ghost, but
the only death in her arms
is her mother's.

You broke it.

She looks so much like her mother, who looked
so much like her father, who looked like his mother, before.
Suicide runs in this family. He sees it tucked behind
George's ear like an heirloom.

He says,
I'm not here to be anyone's friend. There's a system.

Putting the boat back together takes patience.
The old wood splinters in his hands and it—it hurts.
It's never hurt before.

Your system's broken.

Oh, he hates her.
My boat's broken. It's not the same thing.

Q&A

George, of course, has no point of reference for the typical time-line of the building of boats. But people are dying all the time and so the boatman must be able to build faster than this. There must be other boats. Or else he's put the souls of half the world on hold while he saws away at this one. It doesn't seem very responsible.

I build until it's finished.

Except that doesn't make any sense, because what if whoever it's for dies in the meantime, and then what happens? Where does their soul go? Do they sit around in limbo for the rest of forever, waiting for their ticket to the afterlife? Is there some spectral waiting room where souls just sit around twiddling their ecto-thumbs until their number gets called? Is being dead like a never-ending trip to the DMV? Going to the DMV has always kind of felt like dying.

It doesn't work like that, George.

Whoever it's for must be important, if their boat is so complicated. It must be something special for it to take so long.

I've carried kings in boats smaller than this.

Maybe kings aren't that important.

THE VOICEMAIL
George's father left on her phone the night her mother died

George? Georgie? It's—it's Dad. There's been—oh, jesus christ. There's, uh.

You need to come home, Georgie. I need—it's your mom, George. She... I wasn't fast enough, baby, I couldn't stop her, I wasn't even home—I didn't know. I'm so sorry. I'm so, so sorry.

She did it. She finally did it. And I can't—

In the closet. In the fucking hallway closet.

She loved you so much, baby. She loved you so much and I love you so much and I'm sorry I wasn't the man you needed me to be—the man you both needed me to be, I'm so sorry. I never thought—

I never thought she'd really do it, you know? And I'm listening, now. I'm finally fucking listening and I promise I'll always believe you. I'll always believe you, I just need you to come home. Georgie. Georgie, I love you, I just need you to—

[voicemail box full]

AFTER HER MOTHER

Where do you put the pieces of a broken father?

George comes home. She does her best to stack him up
in the shape of a man, to fire him into a stained glass window.
He as all the right parts: two legs, two arms, an albeit broken
heart. But he just isn't quite—finished.

She doesn't push her own mourning onto him.
Someone has to hold the place together and George is good
at holding things together. Even fathers.

Problem solving runs in the family, too.
George's particular brand of epoxy looks like
phone calls and funeral arrangements and never having
to look at the dead, blue face her father came home to.
She asks for a closed casket and doesn't let herself think
about how many years it's been since she's actually
seen her mother.

George's particular brand of "keep going" involves
washing the sheets and cleaning out the closet
and quietly imagining the moment
where she swims too far out to sea

and lets the blue into her lungs.

THE SUICIDE NOTE THAT DOESN'T LOOK LIKE ONE

George's mother never left a note.
George promises that if she has to leave her father,
it won't be with nothing. She has seen
what that nothing looks like in his body and
the way it eats at him.

She throws away the note in the bottom of her dresser
and writes a new one.

Dad,
I need a new start. I'm sorry to go and leave when you need me,
but I can't take another day in this town. I booked a plane to Europe.
I promise I'll call when I get set up, over there.
I'll even pay for the international minutes.
I love you.

Georgie
P.S. – Mom wasn't your fault, Dad.
She really wasn't.
I promise.
Thank you for listening.

INTO THE BLUE

The ocean feels like ice, this far north.
It wraps its fingers around George's ankles,
foam kissing her calves. Her toes have gone numb.

She isn't sure how long she's been standing here,
holding the surf against her skin, but the moon hangs
like a chandelier with all those stars.
With white light reflecting off the water, it's hard to tell
where the black sky stops and the black sea starts.
Maybe, if she wades out far enough,
she'll find out how the earth looks
from outer space.

Two steps.

The water at her thighs, now:
her skirt billowed around her,
seaweed tied around her ankles.

Two more.

Water at her waist, the tide strong enough
to rock her backward, then forward,
toes sinking into the sand,
heels dragging over it.

Two steps.

Water to her chest.
The cold feels real, now~
the kind of cold that hurts.
The kind of cold that sinks into your bones.
She sucks in a breath that's too close
to a gasp.
She is not afraid.
She is not afraid.

Two more.

Water to her throat.
Water to her chin.
Water so high she has to tip her head back
to keep from swallowing it.
Seaweed on her ankles, her knees, her thighs.
The tide lifting her up onto her toes,
into a stumble, a tug at her feet trying to
drag her out to sea.

Two steps.

A hand around her wrist.
A yank backwards.

THE BOATMAN'S MONOLOGUE or
ANGER IS A SECONDARY EMOTION or
I'D RATHER SCARE YOU AWAY THAN FERRY YOU ACROSS THE STYX

WHAT DO YOU THINK YOU'RE DOING?
I know everything that happens in this water; did you think I
wouldn't notice? Did you think you could slip past me? That I'd
build your boat without knowing what you'd done?
All that life. All that breath *and you don't even want it. Do you*
have any idea what I could do with a life like that? The
kingdoms I could burn to the ground? All I'd need is a proper
heartbeat and I could build a legacy. And what good is that body
to you? You're just wasting it. Nearly three decades free to come
and go as you choose and what do you have to show for it? But
I—oh, I would do so well in your skin.
I was a god once, little girl.
I could crawl into your ribcage and wear you like a suit: sit
behind your teeth while you creak and settle like an old house. I
could trap you in this eternity with me—drag you through the
centuries on a leash. You, with all this time and me, with all
that belonging. They would see *me. They'd finally see me.*
My voice would be like music in your mouth and I'd use it so
much better than you did. It'd be easy to open your skull and
make a nest in all your brain-matter. You want to die?
I'll give you a reason to be fascinated with death.

YOU DON'T SCARE ME, BOATMAN. I AM NOT AFRAID OF
THE RIVER STYX.

YOU SHOULD BE.

I trust you.

BE AFRAID OF ME.

No.

I DON'T WANT YOU.

Why not? Why am I special?

YOU'RE NOT. YOU'RE NOT SPECIAL.
YOU'RE SO UNREMARKABLE.

(for the first time in three thousand years, the boatman weeps.)

HOW TO COMFORT A MAN WHO HAS NEVER BEEN HUMAN ENOUGH TO FEEL SORROW

The dead often cry.
Even without bodies, their souls remember.
They sit in his boats and weep for things
he wouldn't know how to call by name.
He had no idea it hurt so much.
George brings with her so much aching.

She asks,
Do you wish you were alive? Really alive? Not tied to the river.

Her hand on his back is warm;
he can't remember ever knowing what warm felt like.
All at once, it's so obvious that she is this
beacon of heat
and light
and life
and he
is so cold.

I'm jealous of all of you.

She says,
*You know, boatman, I think we get along so well
because we're the same kind of unhappy.*

The tide kisses the docks. When was the last time
he left this shore? How many hundreds of years since
Greece? Since Zeus and Hera? Since Olympus fell
and he was abandoned to an eternity of working
for no god?

The lungs he's never used have crawled up into his throat.
Choking on them, he asks,
What do you do when you're unhappy?

Her arm around his shoulder, this is the closest
he has ever felt to being alive and he's crying.

Looking at the sea instead of him, she says:
You live with it.

What a tender way to be born.

WORD OF MOUTH #4

Instead of a bedtime story, George's grandmother tells her,
They say he's a devil. An evil spirit. They say
nothing will ever grow on the ground where
he walks.

The old fisherman died, last week. They put pennies on his eyes
so the boatman would ferry his soul into the deep.
Turns out, forever isn't so expensive.
Turns out, his fee is the most you'll ever pay.

Big Jimmy swears he saw that old fisherman, the other day.
Swears he was captaining a boat just as surely as he ever had.
Like he could leave this world, but not the sea.

Madi Mae says,
I don't go to those docks, anymore. It's too cold, there.
I look at the water and don't see nothing but death.

FINISHED

After all that work, the boat looks so unremarkable:
seated in the sand by the shoreline, its dark wood
polished to a sheen.
Unused.

For the first time in three thousand years,
the boatman wonders if it's possible
to outrun death.

KHARON, OF THE RIVER

George finds him sitting in the sand, staring.

It's just a boat. Too big, sure. Too wide.
But hardly special.

For a while, the only moving thing is the ocean.
She stands. He sits. They say nothing
while the silence goes taut and thin as spider silk.
No one ever came.

He says,
There used to be just one,
in the beginning.
Mine.
But after Olympus fell, the Styx... changed.
Grew hungry. Lost souls drowned my boat in the undertow
and warned me never to return.
The river I pledged my immortal soul to
and it stranded me.

She sits down beside him.
You hate it here.
Her sympathy feels soft and strange.
Who pities death? Who's ever needed to?

His throat goes traitorously tight, voice all wet
and wrecked in the way it never used to be, because
he never used to use his mouth to speak.
I was not made for here.

PAST, PRESENT, FUTURE

You never took the childhood I kept for you.

What would I do with it?

What do you mean?

I... outgrew it. Sure, it's beautiful,
but it's not me anymore.
Why did you keep it?

It reminds me of the Styx. Youth. Light.

I thought the Styx was old?

Compared to you.

Touche.
So—what happened to the dead before
you showed up? I mean, you haven't
been here forever, have you?
Where did they used to go?

They found another way to pass over.
I imagine they'll do the same when I'm gone.

Gone?

Immortality is tricky.
The pantheon I was born under
fell from power and was lost, centuries ago.
I'm nothing but the crater they left
in the ground. Someday,
the world will spin forward and I
will cease to matter.

And the souls?

Will go on as they always do.
What I do is important. For now.
But I'm only a middleman to eternity.

A silence.
George stands up.
She climbs into the boat.

INTO THE BLUE PT 2

For the boatman, fear feels like this:
all Earth's gravity thrown into reverse.
His body in free fall, hurtling towards the Styx.
Cracking ice on a frozen ocean.
A tornado on the inside of his mouth,
plucking up teeth.

GET AWAY FROM THERE.
He shakes.
He does not use his lips to speak.

It's not too big.
Her smile, a sunrise in miniature:
the whole of Olympus reflected in her eyes.
She feels so familiar.
It's built for two.

The heart he didn't know he had beats against his ribs,
making a war drum of his body.
I can't go back to the Styx.

So we go somewhere else. Anywhere else.
George has never feared death. Even less so
with the reaper's right hand man beside her.
But this—this isn't a slow motion suicide.
This
could be a future.

The boatman doesn't know how to say "I'm scared,"
so instead, he says,
It's dark.

Beside the boat, nestled in the sand,
sit two mason jars flooded with light:
pearls of childhood drifting aimlessly as fireflies.
In George's hold, they hum to life—
bump against the glass to try and kiss her hands.
They've missed her.

When she ties them to the bow of the ship,
they are the softest lanterns, pointing like a compass
into the deep.

Are you coming?

The boatman hesitates.
He has been in this business for longer
than anyone can remember.
He has met everyone
who has ever mattered and
everyone who will ever matter and
everyone who won't.

He drags the boat
into the water.

They go.

WORD OF MOUTH #5

Madi Mae says,
The clouds broke over the docks the other day.
First time I ever seen sunshine there.
All that blue water, blue sky.
It was something beautiful.

Big Jimmy says,
Water's been calm for weeks. Smooth sailin'.
Don't see those boats no more. The ones
with no captains? I figure
whoever or whatever was making 'em
finally found some sorta peace.

George's father says,
There's too much space in this old house.

The old fisherman's daughter picks up where he left off.
She patches up his boat, buys new nets, new equipment. Says,
This place had all sorts of legends, ghost stories.
But my papa loved these waters.
I figure I should, too.

POSTSCRIPT

When the boat hits land
George calls her father,
just like she said she would
in the promise
she never expected
she'd be keeping.

When they stumble into tears
which stumble into laughter
it feels like an apology.
It feels like a beginning.

44

46

ACKNOWLEDGMENTS

To Jack Heifner, the theatrical sweetheart who first laid eyes on this when it was still a stage play. And for every time in playwrighting classes when he told me to give the story what it needs—turns out this one needed poetry.

To my sister, for always having my back when I show up at all hours of the night asking for art for my books.

To my best friend and all the courage he comes with.

To Chris Diaz—his gentle patience, his unending light.

To Trista Mateer, who convinced me this weird little project was worth trying.

To Caitlyn Siehl, who convinced me *poetry* was worth trying.

To my father, who spent his life painting the ocean. This story was the last thing we ever talked about. I hope you find your way to it.

To you. All of you. This book means everything to me. Thank you for believing in it. Drag your boats into the water.

And go.

48

ABOUT THE AUTHOR

Ashe Vernon is a queer writer currently stationed in Austin, Texas. Their previous collections of poetry were published through Words Dance Publishing and Where Are You Press. Typically, they spend summers touring poetry with their best friend, hoping no one will notice that they're really just a swarm of bees in a trench coat.

You can find more poetry at latenightcornerstore.com or get in contact at ashevernonpoetry@yahoo.com

Printed in Great Britain
by Amazon